GERMAN

Peter Ec'
Hermu
Illustrated by J

Designed by Graham Round
Edited by Susan Meredith

Contents

First published in 1982 by Usborne Publishing Ltd, Usborne House 83-85 Saffron Hill, London EC1N 8RT, England.
Copyright © 1987, 1982 Usborne Publishing Ltd.

The name Usborne and the device 🐝 are Trade Marks of Usborne Publishing Ltd.

Printed in Britain.

How to use this Book

This book will help you make yourself understood in most everyday situations when you are on holiday or travelling in Germany. The phrases have been kept as simple as possible, and include some of the possible answers to the questions you may want to ask. There are also translations of many of the signs you will see.

On the next two pages, you will find out how to use the pronunciation guide and there are some useful hints and phrases to remember. At the back of the book you can find some very basic German grammar, including a few common verbs.

The book is divided into sections, each covering a situation you are likely to find yourself in. Use the contents list at the front or the index at the back to help you find the pages you need. You will find it easier if you look up the section you are going to need in advance, so you can practise saying the phrases.

For most phrases, there is a picture with a speech bubble containing the German. Underneath the picture is a guide to help you pronounce the German and an English translation. Like this:

Ikh shprekka doitsh.
I can speak German.

Points to remember

We have not always had enough space to include the words for "please" (*bitte*), or "excuse me" (*Entschuldigung*). Try to remember to add them when you are asking for things.

Bitte

There are three words in German for "you" – *du, ihr* and *Sie. Du* (singular) and *ihr* (plural) are used by close friends and children. *Sie* is for speaking to people you don't know very well. Be careful about using *du* or *ihr*, as people may think you are being rude.

Du or Sie?

Pronunciation Guide

We have tried to keep the pronunciation guides in this book as simple as possible. For each German sound we have used the English word, or part of a word, which sounds most like it. Read the pronunciation guide in what seems to be the most obvious way. It will sound better if you say it quickly, so it is a good idea to practise a bit. People should be able to understand what you are saying, even if you won't sound quite like a German person. If you want to learn really good pronunciation you should try to find a German person to teach you.

Here are some general points to remember when you are trying to speak German.

ch

In German "ch" is a soft sound made in the very back of the throat, like the sound at the end of the Scottish word "loch". We have used "kh" for it in the pronunciation guide.

sch

"Sch" in German is always pronounced "sh", as in the English word "ship".

The German "w" is pronounced like an English "v".

w

The German "v" is pronounced like an English "f".

v

g

The German "g" is usually pronounced as in the English word "get". The exceptions are after the letter "n", when it is sometimes pronounced as in "long", and at the end of a word, when it is usually pronounced like the German "ch" ("kh").

a ä

The German "a" is usually a short sound, as in the English word "cat". Where it has to be lengthened, as in the English word "bark", we have shown it as "ar" in the pronunciation guide. "Ä" is pronounced like the "e" in "egg".
"Au" is pronounced like the "ow" in "owl". Whenever you see "ow" in the pronunciation guide, say it like this. "Äu" and "eu" are both pronounced like the "oi" in "oil".

u ü

The German "u" is pronounced as in the English word "put". To make the German "ü" sound, try saying the English word "ewe" quickly with your lips pursed.

The German "ö" is pronounced like the "er" in the English word "fern".

ö

German "ei" is pronounced like the English word "eye".

ei

In German "ie" is pronounced "ee" as in the English word "feel".

ie

Some Basic Words and Phrases

Here are some useful words and phrases which you will need in all kinds of situations.

Ja	Nein
Yah	Nine
Yes	**No**
Bitte	Danke
Bitta	Danka
Please	**Thank you**

Guten Tag
Gooten Targ
Hello

Auf Wiedersehen
Owf veeder-zayen
Goodbye

Tut mir leid
Toot meer light
I'm sorry

Entschuldigung
Ent-shuldigung
Excuse me

Herr
Hair
Mr

Frau
Frow
Mrs

Fräulein
Froi-line
Miss

Some simple questions

How much?	Wieviel?
	Vee-feel?
How many?	Wie viele?
	Vee-feela?
Why?	Warum?
	Var-um?
Which one?	Welcher (cha, ches)?
	Velkh-yer (ya, yez)?
Where is . . .?	Wo ist . . .?
	Vo ist . . .?
When?	Wann?
	Van?
Have you . . .?	Haben Sie . . .?
	Harben zee . . .?
Is (are) there . . .	Gibt es . . .?
	Gibt ess . . .?

Some simple statements

I am . . .	Ich bin . . .
	Ikh bin . . .
I have . . .	Ich habe . . .
	Ikh harba . . .
It is . . .	Das ist . . .
	Dass ist . . .
It is here.	Das ist hier.
	Dass ist here.
It is there.	Das ist dort.
	Dass ist dort.
Over there.	Da drüben.
	Dah drewben.
This one.	Dies hier.
	Deess here.
That one.	Das da.
	Dass dah.
I would like . . .	Ich möchte . . .
	Ikh merkhta . . .

Problems with the language

Do you speak English?
Sprechen Sie Englisch?
Shprekhen zee en-glish?

I do not speak German.
Ich spreche kein Deutsch.
Ikh shprekha k-eye-n doitsh.

I do not understand you.
Ich verstehe Sie nicht.
Ikh fair-shtaya zee nikht.

Please speak more slowly.
Langsamer bitte.
Langzarmer bitta.

What does that mean?
Was bedeutet das?
Vass be-doitet dass?

5

Finding your Way

Wie komme ich bitte zum Bahnhof?

Vee. komma ikh bitta tsoom barnhoaf?
How do I get to the railway station, please?

Du mußt den 6er Bus nehmen.

Doo musst dane zexer booss naymen.
You must take a number 6 bus.

Wo hält der Bus zum Bahnhof?

Das ist da drüben.

Vo hellt dare booss tsoom barnhoaf?
Where is the bus stop for the station?

Dass ist dah drewben.
Over there. It's that one.

Ist hier irgendwo eine Bank?

Ist here eer-gentvo eye-na bank?
Is there a bank near here?

Wo ist das Schloß?

Vo ist dass shloss?
Where is the castle?

Ich habe mich verirrt. Wie heißt diese Straße?

Ikh harba mikh fair-eert. Vee highst deeza shtrarsa? **I'm lost. What is the name of this street.**

Können Sie es mir auf dem Plan zeigen?

Kernen zee ess meer owf dame plan ts-eye-gen?
Can you show me on the map?

General directions

Rechts abbiegen.
Rekhts ap-beegen.
Turn right.

Links abbiegen.
Links ap-beegen.
Turn left.

Immer geradeaus.
Immer gerarda-ows.
Go straight on.

Es ist gegenüber vom Kino.
Ess ist gaygen-ewber fom keeno.
It's opposite the cinema.

Es ist neben der Bank.
Ess ist nayben dare bank.
It's next to the bank.

Es ist an der Ecke.
Ess ist an dare ekka.
It's on the corner.

Es ist direkt hinter der Brücke.
Ess ist deer-ekt hinter dare brukka.
It's just after the bridge.

Es ist direkt vor der Kreuzung.
Ess ist deer-ekt for dare kroits-ung.
It's just before the crossroads.

Some places to ask for

Polizeiamt
pollits-eye-amt
police station

Bahnhof
barnhoaf
railway station

Kinderspielplatz
kinder-shpeel-plats
children's playground

Flughafen
floog-harfen
airport

Geschäfte
geshefta
shops

7

At the Railway Station

If you are under 12 you only pay half fare. Sometimes you have to pay a supplementary charge to travel on a fast train over only a short distance. People under 23 can buy a monthly "Tramper" ticket, which allows them to go anywhere in the country.

Wo kauft man die Fahrkarten?

Vo kowft man dee far-karten?
Where can I buy a ticket?

Wieviel kostet es nach Frankfurt?

Vee-feel kostet ess nakh Frankfoort?
How much is it to Frankfurt?

Eine einfache Fahrkarte nach Frankfurt.

Eye-na eye-n-fakha far-karta nakh Frankfoort.
One single ticket to Frankfurt.

Zwei Rückfahrkarten nach Frankfurt.

Tsv-eye Rukfar-karten nakh Frankfoort.
Two return tickets to Frankfurt.

Von welchem Bahnsteig fährt der Zug nach Frankfurt?

Bahnsteig 5.

Fon velkhem barn-sht-eye-g fairt dare tsoog nakh Frankfoort?
Which platform does the Frankfurt train leave from?
Barn-sht-eye-g funf.
Platform 5.

Um wieviel Uhr fährt der Zug ab?

Um vee-feel ooa fairt dare tsoog ap?
What time does the train leave?

Ist das der Zug nach Frankfurt?

Ist dass dare tsoog nakh Frankfoort?
Is this the Frankfurt train?

Ich habe meine Fahrkarte verloren!

Ikh harba miner far-karta fair-loren!
I've lost my ticket!

Um wieviel Uhr kommt der Zug aus München an?

Um vee-feel ooa kommt dare tsoog ows Munkhen an?
What time does the train from Munich arrive?

Wo sind die Gepäckkarten?

Vo zint dee ge-pek-karten?
Where can I find a luggage trolley?

Information

Luggage collection

Waiting room

Lost property

Departures   **Arrivals**

Left luggage

Not drinking water

Do not lean out of the window

Travelling by Car

Wo ist die nächste Tankstelle?

Vo ist dee nexta tank-shtella?
Where is the nearest garage?

Wieviel Benzin wollen Sie?

Vee-feel bentseen vollen zee?
How much petrol do you want?

Voll, bitte.

Foll, bitta.
Fill it up, please.

Können Sie Öl und Wasser kontrollieren?

Kernen zee erl unt vasser kontrolleeren?
Can you check the oil and water?

Ich habe eine Panne.

Ikh harba eye-na panna.
I have broken down.

Was ist denn kaputt?

Vass ist den kaputt?
What's the trouble?

Die Bremsen funktionieren nicht richtig.

Dee bremsen funkts-yon-eeren nikht rikhtikh.
The brakes are not working properly.

Ich möchte ein Auto für diese Woche mieten.

Ikh merkhta eye-n owtoe foor deeza vokha meeten.
I would like to hire a car for the week.

Parts of the car

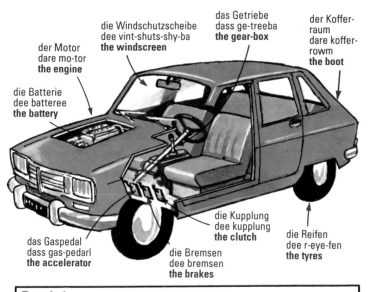

die Windschutzscheibe
dee vint-shuts-shy-ba
the windscreen

das Getriebe
dass ge-treeba
the gear-box

der Koffer-
raum
dare koffer-
rowm
the boot

der Motor
dare mo-tor
the engine

die Batterie
dee batteree
the battery

die Kupplung
dee kupplung
the clutch

das Gaspedal
dass gas-pedarl
the accelerator

die Bremsen
dee bremsen
the brakes

die Reifen
dee r-eye-fen
the tyres

Road signs

Crossroad or junction
where you must give
way to traffic coming
from right

Give way

Customs

One way street

You have right of way
over cars coming in
from side roads

You no longer have
right of way

Town sign

Speed limit

Recommended
speed

11

At the Hotel

You can get a list of hotels from the local tourist office (*Verkehrsamt*), who will book rooms in advance for you. Every hotel room contains a notice showing the price of the room. Some hotels are in old castles and palaces. You can find out about these from the German National Tourist Office.

Booking in advance

Ich möchte ein Zimmer für nächste Woche reservieren.

Ikh merkhta eye-n tsimmer foor nexta vokha rez-air-veeren.
I would like to book a room for next week.

Finding a room

Es tut mir leid, das Hotel ist voll.

Ess toot meer light, dass hotel ist foll.
I'm sorry, but the hotel is full.

Können Sie mir ein anderes Hotel empfehlen?

Kernen zee meer eye-n anderez hotel emp-fay-len?
Can you recommend another hotel?

Ein Zweibettzimmer.

Eye-n tsv-eye-bet-tsimmer.
A room with two beds.

Ein Doppelzimmer mit Bad.

Eye-n doppel-tsimmer mit bart.
A double room with bathroom.

Ein Einzelzimmer mit Dusche.

Eye-n eye-ntsel-tsimmer mit doosha.
A single room with shower.

Wie lange wollen Sie bleiben?

Vee langa vollen zee bl-eye-ben?
How long will you be staying?

Hotel meals

Preisliste
Price-lista
Tariff

Vollpension
Foll-penss-yone
Full board

Zimmer mit
Frühstück
Tsimmer mit
Froo-shtook
Bed and breakfast

Halbpension
Halp-penss-yone
Half-board

Um wieviel Uhr gibt es Frühstück (Mittagessen, Abendessen)?

Um vee-feel ooa gibt ess froo-shtook (mittarg-essen, arbent-essen)?
What time is breakfast (lunch, dinner) served?

Brötchen
Brertkhen
Rolls

Gekochtes Ei
Ge-kokhtez eye
Boiled egg

Schinken
Shinken
Ham

Kaffee
Kaffay
Coffee

Könnten Sie mir ein Eßpaket machen?

Kernten zee meer eye-n ess-pakayt makhen?
Could you make me a packed lunch?

Meinen Schlüssel, bitte.

Welche Zimmernummer haben Sie?

Mine-en shlussel, bitta.
My key, please.

Velkha tsimmer-nummer harben zee?
What is your room number?

Ich möchte eine Nachricht für meinen Bruder hinterlassen.

Ikh merkhta eye-na nakhrikht foor mine-en brooder hinter-lassen.
I would like to leave a message for my brother.

Paying the bill

Machen Sie mir bitte die Rechnung?

Makhen zee meer bitta dee rekhnung.
My bill, please.

Going Camping

There are about 2,000 campsites in Germany. Most have good facilities and many are in beauty spots. Most of the campsites are open from May to September and some, in winter sports areas, are also open in winter. You can get a list of sites from the German National Tourist Office

Finding a campsite

Kann man hier campen?

Kann man here campen?
May we camp here?

Gibt es hier in der nähe einen Campingplatz?

Gibt ess here in dare naya eye-nen camping-plats?
Is there a campsite near here?

Wir haben einen Wohnwagen und zwei Zelte.

Veer harben eye-nen vone-vargen unt tsv-eye tselta.
We have a caravan and two tents.

At the campsite

Wir möchten eine Woche bleiben.

Veer merkhten eye-na vokha bl-eye-ben.
We would like to stay for a fortnight.

Haben Sie einen schattigen Platz?

Harben zee eye-nen shattigen plats?
Have you a shady place?

Sind hier noch andere englische Familien?

Zint here nokh andera en-glisha fameel-yen?
Are there any other English families here?

Um wieviel Uhr machen Sie abends zu?

Um vee-feel ooa makhen zee arbents tsoo?
What time do you close in the evenings?

Wo kann ich mich waschen?

Vo kann ikh mikh vashen?
Where can I wash?

Wo gibt es hier Wasser?

Vo gibt ess here vasser?
Where can I find some water?

Darf ich mir mal Ihre Taschenlampe leihen?

Darf ikh meer marl eera tashen-lampa l-eye-en?
May I borrow your torch?

Dürfen wir hier ein Lagerfeuer machen?

Doorfen veer here eye-n laager-foier makhen?
Are we allowed to make a campfire?

Was ist das für ein Geruch?

Vass ist dass foor eye-n gerookh?
What is that smell?

Könnten Sie bitte ein bißchen weniger Lärm machen?

Kernten zee bitta eye-n biss-yen vain-igger lairm makhen?
Please, could you make less noise?

What the signs mean

GESCHIRR ABWASCHEN VERBOTEN
No washing up in the basins

AUTOS HIER PARKEN
Compulsory parking

TRINKWASSER
Drinking water

NUR FÜR WOHNWAGEN
Caravans only

DIE CAMPER WERDEN GEBETEN, DIE ABFALLKÖRBE ZU BENUTZEN
Campers are requested to dispose of their rubbish in the places provided

Going Shopping

German shops are usually open from 9 a.m. to 6 p.m. during the week and from 8.30 a.m. to 12 or 1 p.m. on Saturdays. On the first Saturday of the month they are also open in the afternoon. In smaller towns the shops may be closed for a couple of hours at lunchtime.

Wo kann ich Obst kaufen?

Vo kann ikh oabst kowfen?
Where can I buy some fruit?

Haben Sie Äpfel?

Harben zee epfel?
Have you any apples?

Wieviel möchten Sie?

Ein Kilo.

Vee-feel merkhten zee?
How many would you like?

Eye-n keeloe.
A kilo.

Vier Scheiben Schinken bitte.

Fear sh-eye-ben shinken bitta.
Four slices of ham, please.

Ich gucke nur.

Ikh kukka noor.
I'm just looking.

Signs

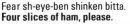

Ausverkauf

Sale

Selbstbedienung

Self-service

AUFZUG

Lift

Von 10 bis 16 Uhr geöffnet

Open from 10 a.m. to 4 p.m.

Buying clothes

> Könnten Sie mir helfen? Ich suche eine gemusterte Bluse.

> Ja. Welche Größe möchten Sie?

Kernten zee meer helfen? Ikh zookha eye-na ge-musterta blooza.
Can you help me? I'm looking for a patterned shirt.

Yah. Velkha grersa vunshen zee?
Yes. What size do you want?

> Kann ich sie anprobieren?

Kann ikh zee anprobeeren?
May I try it on?

Das ist zu groß.

Das ist zu klein.

Dass ist tsoo gross.
It's too big.

Dass ist tsoo kl-eye-n.
It's too small.

> Wieviel kostet das?

Vee-feel kostet dass?
How much is it?

> Haben Sie etwas Billigeres?

Harben zee etvass billigerez?
Have you anything cheaper?

> Wo muß ich bezahlen?

Vo muss ikh be-tsarlen?
Where do I pay?

> Danke.

> Nichts zu danken.

Danka.
Thank you.

Nikhts tsoo danken.
You are welcome.

Ikh merkhta . . .
I would like . . .

LEBENSMITTEL

Laybensmittel **Grocer**

Konserven
kon-sair-ven
some tinned foods

Käse
kayza
some cheese

Butter
butter
some butter

Eier
eye-yer
some eggs

Marmelade
marmelarda
some jam

Tee
tay
some tea

Zucker
tsukker
some sugar

Kekse
keksa
some biscuits

Milch
milkh
some milk

Honig
hoan-ikh
some honey

Senf
senf
some mustard

grüne Bohnen
grewna bone-en
some green beans

Kaffee
kaffay
some coffee

Erbsen
airbsen
some peas

ein Blumenkohl
eye-n bloomen-coal
a cauliflower

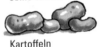

Kartoffeln
kartoffeln
some potatoes

ein Kopfsalat
eye-n kopf-salart
a lettuce

Pilze
piltsa
some mushrooms

ein Kohlkopf
eye-n coal-kopf
a cabbage

Tomaten
tomarten
some tomatoes

Zwiebeln
tsvee-beln
some onions

Himbeeren
him-bair-en
some raspberries

Äpfel
epfel
some apples

Birnen
beer-nen
some pears

eine Apfelsine
eye-na apfel-zeena
an orange

eine Zitrone
eye-na tsit-roan-a
a lemon

Erdbeeren
airt-bair-en
**some
strawberries**

Bananen
bananen
**some
bananas**

Pflaumen
pflowmen
some plums

FLEISCHEREI

Fl-eye-sher-eye
Butcher

Steak
Shtayk
Steak

Frankfurters
Frankfoorters
Frankfurters

Kalbsschnitzel
Kalbs-shnitsel
Veal cutlets

Schweinekoteletts
Shv-eye-na-kotta-lets
Pork chops

Huhn
Hoon
Chicken

Schinken
Shinken
Ham

Salami
Salami
Salami

Wurst
Voorst
Sausage

BÄCKEREI

Bekker-eye
Baker

Vollkornbrot
Foll-korn-broat
Wholemeal bread

Weißbrot
Vice-broat
White bread

Pretzeln
Pretseln
Pretzels

Konditorei

Kondeetor-eye
Cake and sweet shop

Torte
Torta
Gateau

Kuchen
Kookhen
Cake

Obstkuchen
Oabst-kookhen
Fruit tart

Bonbons
Bonbons
Sweets

FISCHGESCHÄFT

Fish gesheft
Fishmonger

Seezunge
Zay-tsunga
Sole

Scholle
Sholla
Plaice

Schokolade
Shokolarda
Chocolate

Pralinen
Praleenen
Chocolates

19

The Shops 2
Buchhandlung · Schreibwaren · Zeitschriften

Bookh-handlung – Shr-eye-bvaren – T-sight-shriften
Bookshop – Stationers – Newsagent

Tinte
tinta
some ink

ein Kugelschreiber
eye-n koogel-shr-eye-ber
a pen

ein Buch
eye-n bookh
a book

ein Radiergummi
eye-n radeer-gummy
a rubber

eine Zeitung
eye-na t-sight-ung
a newspaper

ein Bleistift
eye-n bl-eye-shtift
a pencil

Tabakladen

Tabak-larden
Tobacconist

Schreibpapier
shr-eye-b-papeer
some writing paper

Briefumschläge
breef-umshlayga
some envelopes

ein Feuerzeug
eye-n foier-tsoig
a lighter

eine Schachtel Zigaretten
eye-na shakhtel tsigaretten
a packet of cigarettes

Streichhölzer
shtr-eye-kh-herltser
some matches

Briefmarken
breefmarken
some stamps

Kleiderboutique

Kl-eye-der-booteek
Clothes shop

Shorts
shorts
some shorts

ein Hut
eye-n hoot
a hat

ein Hemd
eye-n hemt
a shirt

ein Rock
eye-n rock
a skirt

ein Kleid
eye-n kl-eye-t
a dress

ein paar Schuhe
eye-n par shooa
some shoes

ein paar Sandalen
eye-n par sandarlen
some sandals

ein Pullover
eye-n pullover
a jersey

ein Badeanzug
eye-n barda-antsoog
a bathing costume

ein Regenmantel
eye-n raygen-mantel
a raincoat

eine Hose
eye-na hoza
some trousers

EISENWARENHANDLUNG

Eye-zenvaren-handlung
Ironmongers – Hardware store

ein Schraubenzieher
eye-n shrowbentsee-er
a screwdriver

ein Korkenzieher
eye-n korken-tsee-er
a corkscrew

ein Dosenöffner
eye-n doze-en-erfner
a tin opener

eine Taschenlampe
eye-na tashen-lampa
a torch

eine Batterie
eye-na batteree
a battery

eine Glühbirne
eye-na gloo-beerna
a light bulb

Bindfaden
bint-farden
some string

Waschmittel
vashmittel
some detergent

Nähgarn
nay-garn
some cotton

eine Nähnadel
eye-na nay-nardel
a needle

ein Stecker
eye-n shtekker
a plug

eine Schere
eye-na shair-a
some scissors

Campinggas
camping-gas
some Camping Gas

Apotheke

Apotayka   **Chemist**

Aspirintabletten
aspireen-tabletten
some aspirin

eine Mullbinde
eye-na mullbinda
a bandage

Insektenspray
insektenspray
some insect repellent

Seife
z-eye-fa
some soap

eine Zahnbürste
eye-na tsarn-boorsta
a toothbrush

Talkumpuder
talkum-pooder
**some talcum
powder**

Zahnpasta
tsarn-pasta
some toothpaste

Pflaster
pflaster
**some sticking
plasters**

ein Kamm
eye-n kamm
a comb

Toilettenpapier
twa-letten-papeer
some toilet paper

ein Film
eye-n film
a film

Posting a Letter

The post office is called the *Postamt*. It is open from 8 a.m. to 6 p.m. on weekdays and from 8 a.m. to midday on Saturdays. Stamps can also often be bought from shops which sell postcards. Postboxes are usually yellow. In towns with airports there are special blue postboxes for airmail.

Wieviel kostet eine Briefmarke für eine Postkarte nach Großbritannien?

Vee-feel kostet eye-na Breefmarka foor eye-na posst-karta nakh gross-britten-yen?
How much is a stamp for a postcard to Great Britain?

Ich möchte vier Briefmarken (für Briefe) nach Großbritannien.

Ikh merkhta fear breefmarken (foor breefa) nakh gross-brittan-yen.
I would like four stamps (for letters) for Great Britain.

Wo gibt es hier einen Briefkasten?

Vo gibt ess here eye-nen breefkasten?
Where can I find a postbox?

The post office

Wo ist das Postamt?

Vo ist dass posst-amt?
Where is the post office?

Ich möchte ein Telegramm nach England schicken.

Ikh merkhta eye-n telegramm nakh en-glant shikken.
I would like to send a telegram to England.

Füllen Sie bitte dieses Formular aus.

Few-len zee bitta deezez form-yoo-lar ows.
Fill in this form, please.

Wieviel kostet es pro Wort?

Vee-feel kostet ess pro vort?
How much is it per word?

...and Changing Money

Wieviel kostet es, dieses Paket nach Großbritannien zu schicken?

Vee-feel kostet ess, deezez pak-ayt nakh gross-brittan-yen tsoo shikken?
How much will it cost to send this parcel to Great Britain?

Um wieviel Uhr geht die letzte Post ab?

Um vee-feel ooa gayt dee letsta posst ap?
What times does the last post leave?

Signs

Air mail

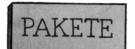

Parcels

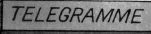

Telegrams

Stamps

Changing money

You can change money and traveller's cheques in a bank, a *bureau de change* and in some hotels and railway stations. Banks are open from 8.30 a.m. to 1.30 p.m. and from 2.30 p.m. to 4 p.m. on weekdays.

Kann ich hier einen Reisescheck eintauschen?

Kann ikh here eye-nen r-eye-za-shek eye-ntowshen?
Can I cash a traveller's cheque here?

Wieviele Deutschmark bekomme ich für ein Pfund?

Vee-feela doitsch-mark bekomma ikh foor eye-n pfunt? **How many deutschmarks are there to the pound?**

Könnten Sie mir Kleingeld geben?

Kernten zee meer kl-eye-ngelt gayben?
Could I have some small change?

23

Going to a Café

You can get a variety of light meals and snacks in German cafés. Both alcoholic and non-alcoholic drinks are served. Many of the cafés have tables outside. Try the German speciality of *Kaffee und Kuchen mit Schlagsahne* (coffee and gateaux with whipped cream).

Ist dieser Tisch besetzt?

Ist deezer tish bezetzt?
Is this table taken?

Was möchten Sie?

Vass merkhten zee?
What can I get you?

Könnten Sie uns bitte die Karte bringen.

Kernten zee unss bitta dee karta bringen?
I would like to see the menu, please.

Was für belegte Brötchen haben Sie?

Wurst, Schinken und Käse.

Vass foor belaygten brertkhen harben zee?
What sandwiches have you got?
Voorst, shinken unt kayza.
Sausage, ham and cheese.

Ich möchte zwei belegte Brötchen mit Schinken, eine Cola und einen Orangensaft.

Ikh merkhta tsv-eye belaygta brertkhen mit shinken, eye-na cola unt eye-nen oranjensaft.
I would like two ham sandwiches, a Coca-Cola and an orange juice.

24

Eine Gabel, bitte.

Eye-na garbel, bitta.
A fork, please.

Das habe ich nicht bestellt.

Dass harba ikh nikht be-shtellt.
This is not what I ordered.

Some things you might need to ask for

ein Messer
eye-n messer
a knife

eine Kanne Wasser
eye-na kanna vasser
a jug of water

ein Löffel
eye-n lerfel
a spoon

ein Glas
eye-n glass
a glass

eine Serviette
eye-na serviette
a napkin

Salz und Pfeffer
salts unt pfeffer
salt and pepper

Wo sind die Toiletten?

Vo zint dee twa-letten?
Where are the toilets?

Bedienung, bitte.

Be-deenung, bitta.
Excuse me, please.

Die Rechnung, bitte.

Dee rekhnung, bitta.
The bill, please.

Ist die Bedienung einbegreifen?

Ist dee be-deenung eyen-be-griffen?
Is service included?

Going to a Restaurant

Most German restaurants serve a variety of regional dishes as well as international food. The menu is usually displayed outside. Look out for *Gasthöfe* (inns) and *Weinstuben* (wine bars). These serve good, simple meals at reasonable prices. A *Bierkeller* is a beer cellar.

Booking a table

Ich möchte für 20 Uhr einen Tisch für vier Personen bestellen.

Ikh merkhta foor tsvantsikh ooa eye-nen tish foor fear pair-zonen be-shtellen.
I would like to book a table for four at 8 p.m.

Haben Sie einen Tisch für vier?

Harben zee eye-nen tish foor fear?
Have you got a table for four?

Haben Sie reserviert?

Harben zee rez-air-veert?
Have you booked?

Haben Sie einen Tisch im Freien?

Harben zee eye-nen tish im fry-en?
Have you a table outside?

Haben Sie sich entschieden?

Harben zee zikh ent-sheeden?
Are you ready to order?

Wie wird dieses Gericht zubereitet?

Vee veert deezez gerikht tsoo-be-r-eye-tet?
How is this dish cooked?

Haben Sie etwas ganz Einfaches?

Harben zee etvass gants eye-nfakh-ez?
Have you got anything very plain?

Drinks

Kann ich die Weinkarte sehen?

Kann ikh dee vine-karta zayen?
Can I see the wine list?

Was empfehlen Sie mir?

Vass empfaylen zee meer?
What do you recommend?

Ich möchte eine Karaffe Wein der Hausmarke und eine flasche Mineralwasser.

Ikh merkhta eye-na karaffa vine dare house-marka unt eye-na flarsha minnerarl-vasser.
I would like a carafe of house wine and a bottle of mineral water.

Was für nichtalkoholische Getränke haben Sie?

Vass foor nikht-alko-hole-ishe ge-trenke harben zee?
What soft drinks have you got?

Entschuldigen Sie, ich habe mein Glas umgekippt.

Ent-shuldigen zee, ikh harba mine glass umgekippt.
I'm sorry, I've spilt my drink.

Wir sind ein wenig in Eile.

Veer zint eye-n vain-ikh in eye-la.
We are in a bit of a rush.

Problems with the bill

Was soll das heißen?

Vass zoll dass h-eye-ssen?
What does this mean?

The Menu

Pumpernickel
Pumpernickel
Dark rye bread

Belegte Brötchen
Be-laygta brertkhen
Sandwiches

Schinken
Shinken
Ham

Käse
Kayza
Cheese

Wurst
Voorst
Sausage

Gemischter Salat
Gemishter Salart
Mixed salad

Kartoffelsalat
Kartoffelsalart
Potato salad

Aufschnitt
Owf-shnitt
Cold meats

Leberkäse
Layberkayza
Meat loaf

Sauerkraut
Sour-krowt
Pickled cabbage

Spätzle
Shpetsla
Noodles

Pfannkuchen
Pfann-kookhen
Pancakes

Schwarzwälderkirschtorte
Shvarts-velder-
keersh-torta
Black Forest gateau

Käsekuchen
Kayza-kookhen
Cheese cake

Eiskrem
Ice-krem
Icecream

Kaffee
Kaffay
Coffee

Tee mit Milch
Tay mit milkh
Tea with milk

Apfelsaft
Apfelsaft
Apple juice

Limonade
Limonarda
Lemonade

Eiskaffee mit Schlagsahne
Ice-kaffay mit shlagzarna
Iced coffee with
        whipped cream

28

Restaurant Menu

Look out for restaurants which have a set menu at lunchtimes. This will be at a fixed price and will work out cheaper than ordering from an *à la carte* menu. Service and VAT will be included in the prices shown on the menu, but wine or beer will be extra.

Speisekarte

Vorspeisen

Forshp-eye-zen
Starters

Geflügelsalat
Ge-floogel-salart
Chicken salad with mayonnaise dressing

Spargel
Shpargel
Asparagus

Gemüsesuppe
Ge-mewza-zuppa
Vegetable soup

Austern
Owstern
Oysters

Hauptgerichte

Howpt-gerikhta
Main courses

Garniertes Sauerkraut
Garneertez sour-krowt
Sauerkraut with sausages and ham

Huhn mit Reis
Hoon mit rice
Chicken with rice

Rheinischer Sauerbraten
Rhine-isher sour-brarten
Rhenish pickled beef

Fisch

Fish
Fish

Blaue Forelle
Bl-owa forella
Trout

Hummer
Hummer
Lobster

Lachs
Lax
Salmon

Gemüse

Ge-mewza
Vegetables

Käseplatte

Kayza-platta
Assorted cheeses

Nachtisch

Nakh-tish
Dessert

Apfelstrudel
Apfel-shtroodel
Apple strudel

Quarkspeise
Kvark-shp-eye-za
Soft cheese dessert with fruit

Obstsalat
Oabst-salart
Fruit salad

Mehrwertsteuer
Mair-vairt-shtoier
V.A.T.

Bedienung einbegreifen
Be-deenung eyen-be-griffen
Service included

Entertainments 1

Many German towns have their own theatre as well as a cinema. To find out what is on, look in a local paper or ask at the nearest tourist office (*Verkehrsamt*). The German National Tourist Office can give you lists of special events in different parts of Germany.

Könnten Sie eine Veranstaltung empfehlen?

Kernten zee eye-na fair-an-shtaltung empfaylen?
Can you recommend a show to see?

Zirkus
Tseer-kuss
Circus

Puppentheater
Puppentay-arter
Puppet theatre

Zeichentrickfilm
Ts-eye-khen-trick-film
Cartoon film

Freilichttheater
Fr-eye-likht-tay-arter
Open-air theatre

Vergnügungspark
Fair-gnew-gungz-park
Funfair

Pantomime
Pantomeema
A pantomime

Licht und Tonschau
Likht unt tone-sh-ow
Sound and light show
(These tell the story of famous old buildings in which they are held.)

Zauberkünstler
Tsowber-kunstler
Magician

Fußballspiel
Fuss-bal-shpeel
Football match

Was gibt es heute abend im Kino?

Gibt es einen Film auf englisch?

Vass gibt ess hoyta arbent im keeno?
What is on at the cinema tonight?

Gibt ess eye-nen film owf en-glish?
Are there any films in English?

Wieviel kosten die Karten?

Zwei Plätze im Parkett.

Vee-feel kosten dee karten?
How much are the tickets?

Tsv-eye pletsa im par-kett.
Two seats in the stalls.

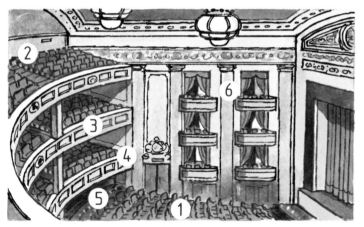

1 Parkett Par-kett **The stalls**	**3** Zweiter Rang Tsv-eye-ter rang **Upper circle**	**5** Sperrsitz Shpair-zitz **Dress circle**
2 Gallerie Gallerree **The gallery**	**4** Erster Rang Airster rang **Lower circle**	**6** Balkon Bal-kone **Boxes**

Entertainments 2

Wann beginnt die Vorstellung?

Van be-ginnt dee for-shtell-ung?
What time does the show begin?

Um 18.30 Uhr. Sie ist um 20.00 Uhr zu Ende.

Um akht-tsayn ooa dry-ssig. Zee ist um tsvantsikh ooa tsoo enda.
At 6.30 p.m. It finishes at 8 o'clock.

Wo kann ich ein Programm kaufen?

Vo kann ikh eye-n pro-gramm kowfen?
Where can I buy a programme?

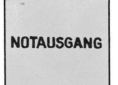

Die Platzanweiserin verkauft Sie.

Dee plats-anv-eye-zerin fair-kowft zee. **The usherette sells them.**

Theatre signs

GARDEROBE

Cloakroom

NOTAUSGANG

Fire exit

TOILETTEN

Toilets

RAUCHEN VERBOTEN

No smoking

Nicht geeignet für Jugendliche unter 18 Jahren

Not suitable for anyone under 18.

Sightseeing 1

You usually have to pay an entrance fee to visit places of interest, but many museums have one free day a week. They are usually open from 10 a.m. to 4 p.m. from Tuesdays to Fridays and in the morning at weekends. They are closed on Mondays and sometimes in winter.

Was gibt es Interessantes in der Stadt?

Vass gibt ess interessantez in dare shtatt?
What is there of interest in the town?

Places to go sightseeing

die Kirche
dee keerkha
the church

das Schloß
dass shloss
the castle

die Altstadt
dee alt-shtatt
the old part of town

der Zoo
dare tsoo
the zoo

der Nationalpark
dare nats-yonarl-park
nature reserve

das Museum
dass moo-zay-um
the museum

die Höhlen
dee herlen
caves

Haben Sie einen Stadtplan?

Harben zee eye-nen shtatt-plan?
Is there a tourist map of the town?

Können Sie mir sagen, wann das Museum geöffnet ist?

Kernen zee meer zargen, vann dass moo-zay-um ge-erfnet ist?
Can you tell me when the museum is open?

Jeden Tag außer montags von 10 bis 16 Uhr.

Yayden targ owsser moan-targz fon tsayn biss zekh-tsayn ooa.
Every day except Monday, from 10 a.m. to 4 p.m.

Wieviel kostet der Eintritt?

Vee-feel kostet dare eye-ntritt?
How much is the admission charge?

33

Sightseeing 2

Guided tours

Gibt es eine Führung auf englisch?

Gibt ess eye-na fewrung owf en-glish?
Is there a guided tour in English?

Ja. Die nächste beginnt in einer Viertelstunde.

Yah. Dee nexta be-ginnt in eye-ner feertel-shtunda.
Yes. The next tour starts in a quarter of an hour.

Wie lange dauert die Führung?

Vee langa dowert dee fewrung?
How long does the tour last?

Kann man auf den Turm steigen?

Kann man owf dane toorm sht-eye-gen?
Are we allowed to go up the tower?

At the zoo

Reptilienhaus
Repteel-yen-house
Reptile house

Vogelhaus
Foe-gel-house
Aviary

Affenhaus
Affen-house
Monkey house

Teeparty der Schimpansen
Teaparty dare shimpansen
Chimpanzees' tea-party

Bärengrube
Bearen-grooba
Bear pit

Eselreiten
Ayzel-rye-ten
Donkey rides

Kamelreiten
Camel-rye-ten
Camel rides

Signs

Do not feed
the animals

Dangerous
animals

Wild animals

Entrance

Exit

Do not touch

Cameras prohibited

Restaurant

Private property

Beware of
the dog

No entrance

Closed for
the holidays

Open

Closed

Keep off
the grass

35

Making Friends

Hallo. Vee highst doo?
Hello. What is your name?

Ikh highsa Karen. Unt doo?
My name is Karen. And yours?

Vo fair-bringst doo diner fairy-en?
Where are you staying?

Ikh vone-a dah drewben.
I live over there.

Vee alt bist doo?
How old are you?

Ikh bin tsverlf.
I'm twelve.

Yah. Ikh harba eye-na eltera shvester, unt deess ist mine tsvillings-brooder.
Yes. I have an elder sister, and this is my twin brother.

Dass ist mine brooder Karl. Hast doo ge-shvister?
Here is my brother Karl. Have you any brothers and sisters?

Kannst doo mit unss tsoo mittarg essen? **Can you have lunch with us?**

Ikh muss miner eltern frargen. **I must ask my parents.**

Gay-en veer shpeelen! **Let's go and play!**

Be-eye-l dikh! **Hurry up!**   Ikh komma! **I'm coming!**   Varta owf mikh! **Wait for me!**

Ikh marg . . . **I like . . .**

Schach
Shakh
Chess

Malen
Marlen
Painting

Briefmarkensammeln
Breef-marken-zammeln
Stamp collecting

Cards

Karo
Karoe
Diamonds

Herz
Hairts
Hearts

Kreuz
Kroits
Clubs

Pik
Peek
Spades

König
Kernikh
King

Dame
Darma
Queen

Bube
Booba
Jack

As
Ass
Ace

Joker
Joker
Joker

Playing Games

Fußball
Fussbal
Football

Versteckenspielen
Fair-shtekken-
shpeelen
Hide and seek

Fang!

Fang!
Catch!

Wer gewinnt?

Wirf mir den Ball!

Himmel und Hölle
Himmel unt herla
Hopscotch

Veerf meer dane bal!
Throw me the ball!

Vair ge-vinnt?
Who is winning?

Murmeln
Moormeln
Marbles

Sport

There is a lot of good fishing in Germany as the country has many lakes, rivers and streams. It is especially good for trout, salmon, pike and carp. You will need a permit (*Angelschein*) to fish. Ask at the nearest tourist office where to get one.

Going fishing

Wo kann ich mir eine Angelrute leihen?

Vo kann ikh meer eye-na an-gel-roota l-eye-en?
Where can I hire a fishing rod?

Wieviel kostet es pro Tag?

Vee-feel kostet ess pro targ?
How much does it cost for the day?

Brauche ich eine Erlaubnis?

Browkha ikh eye-na airl-owbniss?
Do I need a permit?

Verzeihung, haben Sie Köder?

Fairts-eye-ung. Harben zee kerder?
Excuse me, have you any bait?

Ist dies ein guter Angelplatz?

Ist deess eye-n gooter an-gel-plats?
Is this a good place to fish?

Riding

Ist eine Reitschule in der Nähe?

Ist eye-na right-shoola in dare naya?
Is there a riding school near here?

Wir möchten Reitstunden nehmen.

Veer merkhten right-shtunden naymen.
We would like some riding lessons.

40

Skiing

Skistiefel

Ski-shteefel
Ski boots

Skis

Skis
Skis

Stistöcke

Ski-shterka
Ski sticks

Skihandschuhe

Ski-hant-shooa
Ski gloves

Skiausweis

Ski-ows-vice
Ski pass

Wo ist die Skischule?

Vo ist dee ski-shoola?
Where is the ski school?

The ski runs

The ski runs, or *Pisten,* are marked with coloured arrows.

Nursery slopes – very easy.

Beginners – easy.

For quite experienced skiers – quite difficult.

For professional skiers – very difficult.

Ich bin Anfänger.

Ikh bin an-fenger.
I am a beginner.

Ich bin schon einmal skigelaufen.

Ikh bin shoan eye-nmarl ski-ge-lowfen.
I have skied once before.

Ich kann gut skilaufen.

Ikh kann goot ski-lowfen.
I can ski well.

Ich kann nicht aufstehen. Können Sie mir helfen?

Ikh kann nikht owf-shtayen. Kernen zee meer helfen?
I cannot get up. Can you help me?

Wir haben den Weg verloren. Wo ist der Skilift?

Veer harben dane vek fair-loren. Vo ist dare ski-lift?
We are lost. Where is the ski-lift?

At the Seaside 1

Wo ist der nächste Strand?

Vo ist dare nexta shtrant?
Where is the nearest beach?

Gibt es ein Schwimmbad?

Gibt ess eye-n shvimm-bart?
Is there a swimming pool?

Ich möchte zwei Luftmatratzen, einen Liegestuhl . . .

Ikh merkhta tsv-eye luft-matratsen, eye-nen leega-shtool . . .
I would like to hire two mattresses, a deck chair . . .

. . . und einen Sonnenschirm mieten.

. . . unt eye-nen zonnen-sheerm meeten.
. . . and an umbrella.

Wo sind die Umkleidekabinen?

Neben dem Planschbecken.

Vo zint dee um-kl-eye-da-kabeenen?
Where are the changing rooms?
Nayben dame plansh-bekken.
Next to the paddling pool.

Beach things

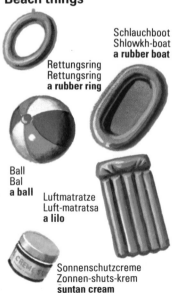

Schlauchboot
Shlowkh-boat
a rubber boat

Rettungsring
Rettungsring
a rubber ring

Ball
Bal
a ball

Luftmatratze
Luft-matratsa
a lilo

Sonnenschutzcreme
Zonnen-shuts-krem
suntan cream

Hallo! Lass unss shvimmen gayen.
Hello! Let's go for a swim.

Kernten zee bitta owf miner zakhen owf-passen?
Please could you look after my things for me?

Pass owf! Dah kommt eye-na grocer vella!
Watch out! There's a big wave coming!

Ist dah eye-na doosha?
Is there a shower?

Gib meer dass hant-tookh.
Pass me the towel.

Wasserski fahren
Vasser-ski far-en
Water skiing

der Strandkorb
dare shtrant-korp
Wind shield

das Segelboot
dass zaygel-boat
Sailing boat

At the Seaside 2

Wollen wir eine Sandburg bauen?

Hast du einen Eimer und Spaten?

Vollen veer eye-na sandboorg bowen.
Shall we build a sandcastle?
Hast doo eye-nen eye-mer unt shparten?
Have you got a bucket and spade?

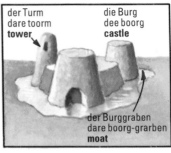

der Turm
dare toorm
tower

die Burg
dee boorg
castle

der Burggraben
dare boorg-grarben
moat

Was bedeutet die rote Flagge?

Vass be-doitet dee rota flagga?
What does the red flag mean?

Es ist gefährlich zu schwimmen. Die See ist zu unruhig.

Ess ist ge-fair-likh tsoo shvimmen. Dee zay ist tsoo unrooikh.
It is dangerous to swim. The sea is too rough.

BADEN VERBOTEN

No Bathing

Mir ist sehr warm.

Meer ist zair varm.
I'm hot.

Lass uns ein Eis kaufen gehen.

Lass unss eye-n ice kowfen gayen.
Let's go and buy an ice cream.

Buying an ice cream

Haben Sie Eis?

Ja. Welchen Geschmack möchtet ihr?

Harben zee ice?
Do you have any ice creams?

Yah. Velkhen ge-shmak merkhtet ear?
Yes. What flavour would you like?

 Vanille
Vanilya
Vanilla

Erdbeere
Airt-bair-a
Strawberry

Himbeere
Him-bair-a
Raspberry

Mokka
Mokka
Coffee

Pistazie
Pistatseea
Pistachio

Schokolade
Shokolarda
Chocolate

Ich möchte ein Vanilleeis.

Ikh merkhta eye-n vanilya-ice.
I would like a vanilla cornet.

Eine oder zwei Kugeln?

Ein Erdbeereis am Stiel.

Eye-na oder tsv-eye koogeln?
A single or a double?

Eye-n airt-bair-ice am shteel.
A strawberry ice lolly.

Wieviel kostet das?

Vee-feel kostet dass?
How much is that?

Zwei Mark.

Danke.

Tsv-eye mark.
Two marks.

Danka.
Thank you.

Accidents and Emergencies

The phone number for the police or ambulance is 110 and for the fire brigade 112. In some boxes, instead of dialling, you push a lever in one direction for the police or ambulance (*Notruf*), in the other for the fire brigade (*Feuerwehr*). Road accidents must be reported to the police.

Hilfe!

Hilfa!
Help!

Kommen Sie schnell!

Kommen zee schnell!
Come quickly!

Feuer!

Foier!
Fire!

Rufen Sie bitte einen Krankenwagen.

Roofen zee bitta eye-nen kranken-vargen.
Please call for an ambulance.

Missing persons

Mein Freund ist seit gestern abend verschwunden.

Mine froint ist sight gestern arbent fair-shvunden.
My friend has been missing since last night.

Wann haben Sie ihn zum letzten Mal gesehen?

Van harben zee een tsoom letsten marl ge-zayen?
When did you last see him?

Er trug eine rote Mütze und ein rotes Halstuch.

Air troog eye-na rota mewtsa unt eye-n rotez halstookh.
He was wearing a red hat and scarf.

Er ging um 6 Uhr abends weg, um eine Zeitung zu kaufen.

Air ging um zex ooa arbents vek, um eye-na t-sight-ung tsoo kowfen.
He went out at 6 o'clock to buy a newspaper.

Lost or stolen

> Ich habe meinen Paß verloren.

Ikh harba mine-en pass fair-loren.
I've lost my passport.

> Meine Brieftasche ist gestohlen worden.

Miner breef-tasha ist ge-shtoe-len vorden. **My wallet has been stolen.**

> Mein Zimmer ist eingebrochen worden.

Mine tsimmer ist eye-n-ge-brokhen vorden.
My room has been burgled.

> Wo können wir Sie erreichen?

Vo kernen veer zee air-eye-khen?
Where can we contact you?

Other things

meine
Reiseschecks
miner
r-eye-za-sheks
**my traveller's
cheques**

mein Fotoapparat
mine photo-apparart
my camera

mein Koffer
mine koffer
my suitcase

meine Schlüssel
miner shlussel
my keys

meine Tasche
miner tasha
my bag

meine Uhr
miner ooa
my watch

> Es passierte zwischen 10 Uhr und Mitternacht.

Ess passeerta tsvishen tsayn ooa unt mitter-nakht.
It happened between 10 o'clock and midnight.

> Hier ist mein Name und meine Adresse.

Here ist mine narma unt miner adressa.
Here is my name and address.

47

Using the Telephone

You will find public phone boxes at post offices and in the street. They take 10 Pfennig, 50 Pfennig, 1 Mark and 5 Mark pieces. To make a local call, lift the receiver, put in two 10 Pfennig pieces and, when you hear the dialling tone, dial the number you want. To make a long distance call you need to find out the area code number. These are listed in a yellow booklet called AVON, which you will find at post offices and in hotels. The booklet also gives the code numbers for places which you can dial direct in foreign countries. If you cannot find the code number for the place you want, phone directory enquiries. The number is 118 or 0118 for places in Germany, and 00118 for places abroad.

Look out for telephone boxes with this green sign on them. It means you can make calls abroad from them.

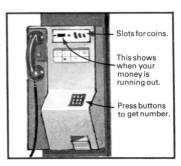

Slots for coins.

This shows when your money is running out.

Press buttons to get number.

Gibt es hier ein öffentliches Telefon?

Gibt ess here eye-n erfentlikhes telefon?
Is there a public telephone here?

Ich möchte ein Rückgespräch nach Köln führen. Die Nummer ist Köln 81269.

Ikh merkhta eye-n ruk-ge-shprekh nakh Kerln fewren. Dee nummer ist Kerln akht eins tsv-eye zex noin.
I want to call Cologne and reverse the charges. The number is Cologne 81269.

Könnten Sie mir bitte Kleingeld geben?

Kernten zee meer bitta kl-eye-ngelt gayben?
Have you got any small change?

Was ist ihre Nummer?
Bleiben Sie am Apparat.

Vass ist eer-a nummer? bl-eye-ben
zee am apparart.
What is your number? Hold the line.

Sie haben die falsche
Nummer gewählt.

Zee harben dee falsha nummer
ge-vairlt. **You have the wrong number.**

Könnte ich bitte mit Herrn
Schmidt sprechen?

Kernta ikh bitta mit hairn Shmitt
shprekhen?
Please may I speak to Mr Schmidt?

Die Nummer ist besetzt.

Dee nummer ist be-zetst.
The number is engaged.

Er ist im Moment nicht
hier.

Wer spricht?

Air ist im mo-mentt nikht here.
He is not here at the moment?

Vair shprikht?
Who is speaking?

Könnten Sie ihm bitte
sagen, daß Jane Brown
angerufen hat und ihn
bitten, diese Nummer
anzurufen?

Kernten zee eem bitta zargen, dass Jane Brown an-ge-roofen hat und een
bitten, deeza nummer an-tsoo-roofen?
**Could you tell him that Jane Brown telephoned and ask him to ring me at
this number?**

Feeling Ill

The *Apotheke* (chemist) will be able to give you advice and medicine for most minor ailments. If you see a doctor you will have to pay him on the spot. Residents of E.E.C. countries can get most of their money refunded when they get home, if they have to pay for hospital or dental treatment.

Ich habe Kopfschmerzen.
Ikh harba kopf-shmairtsen.
I have a headache.

Ich habe Bauchschmerzen.
Ikh harba bowkh-shmairtsen.
I have a stomach pain.

Ich habe mich erkältet.
Ikh harba mikh air-keltet.
I have a cold.

Ich huste viel.
Ikh hoosta feel.
I am coughing a lot.

Ich habe Fieber.
Ikh harba feeber.
I have a temperature.

Mir ist übel.
Meer ist ewbel.
I feel sick.

Ich habe mich geschnitten.
Ikh harba mikh ge-shnitten.
I have cut myself.

Ich habe mich verbrannt.
Ikh harba mikh fair-brannt.
I have burnt myself.

Ich habe einen Sonnenbrand.
Ikh harba eye-nen zonnenbrannt.
I am sunburnt.

Ich bin gestochen (gebissen) worden von . . .
Ikh bin ge-shtokken (ge-bissen) vorden fon . . .
I have been stung (bitten) by . . .

einer Qualle
eye-ner kvarla
a jellyfish

einem Seeigel
eye-nem zay-eagle
a sea-urchin

einer Schlange
eye-ner shlanga
a snake

einer Wespe
eye-ner vespa
a wasp

Ich habe etwas im Auge.
Ikh harba etvass im owga.
I have something in my eye.

Ich habe Ausschlag.
Ikh harba ows-shlarg.
I have a rash.

Es juckt mich.
Ess yukkt mikh.
It itches.

Ich habe Zahn-schmerzen.
Ikh harba tsarn-shmairtsen.
I have toothache.

Ein Hund hat mich angegriffen.
Eye-n hunt hat mikh an-ge-griffen.
I have been attacked by a dog.

Ich habe mir das Bein gebrochen.
Ikh harba meer dass b-eye-n ge-brokhen.
I have broken my leg.

Going to the doctor

Ich brauche einen Arzt.

Ikh browkha eye-nen artst.
I need to see a doctor.

Wann hat er Zeit?

Van hat air t-sight?
When is he free?

Können Sie mich gegen Tetanus impfen?

Kernen zee mikh gaygen tetta-noose impfen?
Can you inoculate me against tetanus?

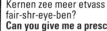

Können Sie mir etwas verschreiben?

Kernen zee meer etvass fair-shr-eye-ben?
Can you give me a prescription?

Parts of the Body

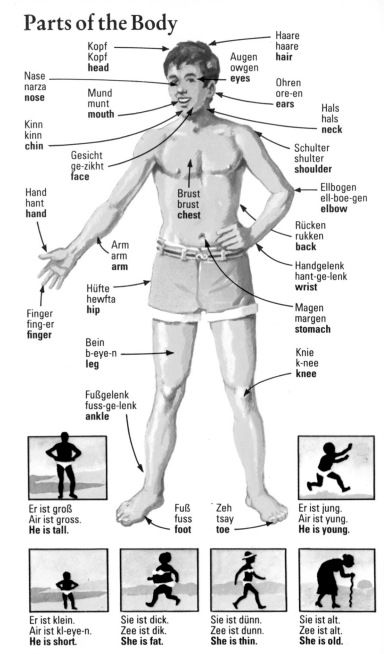

Kopf
Kopf
head

Haare
haare
hair

Augen
owgen
eyes

Nase
narza
nose

Ohren
ore-en
ears

Mund
munt
mouth

Hals
hals
neck

Kinn
kinn
chin

Schulter
shulter
shoulder

Gesicht
ge-zikht
face

Brust
brust
chest

Ellbogen
ell-boe-gen
elbow

Hand
hant
hand

Rücken
rukken
back

Arm
arm
arm

Handgelenk
hant-ge-lenk
wrist

Hüfte
hewfta
hip

Magen
margen
stomach

Finger
fing-er
finger

Bein
b-eye-n
leg

Knie
k-nee
knee

Fußgelenk
fuss-ge-lenk
ankle

Er ist groß
Air ist gross.
He is tall.

Fuß
fuss
foot

Zeh
tsay
toe

Er ist jung.
Air ist yung.
He is young.

Er ist klein.
Air ist kl-eye-n.
He is short.

Sie ist dick.
Zee ist dik.
She is fat.

Sie ist dünn.
Zee ist dunn.
She is thin.

Sie ist alt.
Zee ist alt.
She is old.

52

Colours

Farben (farben)

schwarz
shvarts
black

weiß
vice
white

grau
gr-ow
grey

beige
beige
beige

braun
brown
brown

gelb
gelp
yellow

orange
oranja
orange

rot
rote
red

rosa
rose-a
pink

violett
violett
violet

blau
bl-ow
blue

grün
grewn
green

golden
golden
gold

silbern
zilbern
silver

dunkel
dunkel
dark

hell
hell
light

Months, Seasons and Days

Januar
Yan-yew-ar
January

Februar
Feb-rew-ar
February

März
Mairts
March

April
Apreel
April

Mai
My
May

Juni
Yoonee
June

Juli
Yoolee
July

August
Owgust
August

September
September
September

Oktober
October
October

November
November
November

Dezember
Detsember
December

The week

die Woche (dee vokha)

7	Montag Moan-targ **Monday**	**11**	Freitag Fry-targ **Friday**
8	Dienstag Deens-targ **Tuesday**	**12**	Samstag Zams-targ **Saturday**
9	Mittwoch Mittvokh **Wednesday**	**13**	Sonntag Zonn-targ **Sunday**
10	Donnerstag Donners-targ **Thursday**		

The seasons die Jahreszeiten (dee yarez-t-sight-en)

der Frühling
dare frewling
Spring

der Sommer
dare zommer
Summer

der Herbst
dare hairbst
Autumn

der Winter
dare vinter
Winter

The Weather

Es regnet.
Ess raygnet.
It's raining.

Es wird regnen.
Ess veert raygnen.
It's going to rain.

Es hagelt.
Ess hargelt.
It's hailing.

Es ist windig.
Ess ist vindikh.
It's windy.

Es schneit.
Ess sh-night.
It's snowing.

Es ist bewölkt.
Ess ist be-verlkt.
It's cloudy.

Es donnert.
Ess donnert.
It's thundering.

Ein Blitz.
Eye-n blits.
A flash of lightning.

Was für ein Sturm!
Vass foor eye-n shtoorm!
What a storm!

Es ist schönes Wetter.
Ess ist shernez vetter.
It's a nice day.

Es ist heiß.
Ess ist highss
It's hot.

Es ist kalt.
Ess ist kalt.
It's cold.

Numbers

1 ein(s) / eye-n(s)	16 sechzehn / zekh-tsayn	40 vierzig / fear-tsikh
2 zwei / tsv-eye	17 siebzehn / zeeb-tsayn	50 fünfzig / funf-tsikh
3 drei / dry	18 achtzehn / akht-tsayn	60 sechzig / zex-ikh
4 vier / fear	19 neunzehn / noin-tsayn	70 siebzig / zeeb-tsikh
5 fünf / funf	20 zwanzig / tsvantsikh	80 achtzig / akht-tsikh
6 sechs / zex	21 einundzwanzig / eye-n-unt-tsvantsikh	90 neunzig / noin-tsikh
7 sieben / zeeben	22 zweiundzwanzig / tsv-eye-unt-tsvantsikh	100 hundert / hundert
8 acht / akht	23 dreiundzwanzig / dry-unt-tsvantsikh	101 hunderteins / hundert-eye-nss
9 neun / noin	24 vierundzwanzig / fear-unt-tsvantsikh	200 zweihundert / tsv-eye-hundert
10 zehn / tsayn	25 fünfundzwanzig / funf-unt-tsvantsikh	1,000 tausend / towzent
11 elf / elf	26 sechsundzwanzig / zex-unt-tsvantsikh	1,001 tausendundeins / towzent-unt-eye-nss
12 zwölf / tsverlf	27 siebenundzwanzig / zeeben-unt-tsvantsikh	2,000 zweitausend / tsv-eye-towzent
13 dreizehn / dry-tsayn	28 achtundzwanzig / akht-unt-tsvantsikh	1,000,000 eine Million / eye-na milli-oan
14 vierzehn / fear-tsayn	29 neunundzwanzig / noin-unt-tsvantsikh	1st erster / airster
15 fünfzehn / funf-tsayn	30 dreissig / dry-sikh	2nd zweiter / tsv-eye-ter

The Time

In Germany the 24 hour clock is used, so times after midday are written as 1300, 1400 and so on. Another point to remember is that to say, for example, "it is half past six" in German, you have to say "it is half seven".

Wie spät ist es, bitte?

Vee shpayt ist ess, bitta?
What time is it, please?

Es ist acht Uhr.
Ess ist akht ooa.
It is eight o'clock.

Es ist viertel nach acht.
Ess ist feertel nakh akht.
It is quarter past eight.

Es ist viertel vor neun.
Ess ist feertel for noin.
It is quarter to nine.

Es ist Mittag.
Ess ist mittarg.
It is midday.

Es ist fünf vor fünf.
Ess ist funf for funf.
It is five to five.

Es ist zehn nach sieben.
Ess ist tsayn nakh zeeben.
It is ten past seven.

Es ist halb elf.
Ess ist halp elf.
It is half past ten.

Es ist Mitternacht.
Ess ist mitternakht.
It is midnight.

der Morgen
dare morgen
the morning

der Nachmittag
dare nakh-mittarg
the afternoon

der Abend
dare arbent
the evening

die Nacht
dee nakht
the night

gestern ges-tern **yesterday**	dieses Jahr deezez yar **this year**	früh frew **early**	in fünf Minuten in funf minooten **in five minutes**
heute hoyta **today**	letzten Monat letsten moan-art **last month**	früher frewer **earlier**	in einer Viertelstunde in eye-ner feertel-shtunda **in a quarter of**
morgen morgen **tomorrow**	nächste Woche nexta vokha **next week**	bald balt **soon**	**an hour**
vorgestern vor-ges-tern **the day before yesterday**	jetzt yetst **now**	später shpayter **later**	in einer halben Stunde in eye-ner halben shtunda **in half an hour**
am folgenden Tag am folgenden targ **the following day**		niemals nee-marlz **never**	in einer Stunde in eye-ner shtunda **in an hour**
übermorgen ewber-morgen **the day after tomorrow**		zu spät tsoo spayt **too late**	

Basic Grammar

Nouns

All German nouns are either masculine, feminine or neuter. When you learn a noun, you must learn this as well. The word for "the" is *der* before masculine (m) nouns, *die* before feminine (f) nouns and *das* before neuter (n) nouns.

e.g. *der Hund* (the dog)
die Blume (the flower)
das Kind (the child)

Nouns usually change their endings in the plural (p). Try to learn the plural form at the same time as the singular. When a noun is plural, the word for "the" is *die*.

e.g. *die Hunde* (the dogs)
die Blumen (the flowers)
die Kinder (the children)

All German nouns begin with a capital letter.

The German for "a" or "an" is *ein* before masculine and neuter nouns, and *eine* before feminine nouns.

e.g. *ein Hund* (a dog)
eine Blume (a flower)
ein Kind (a child)

Pronouns

The German word for "it" depends on whether the noun it replaces is masculine, feminine or neuter.

e.g. *der Hund bellt* (the dog barks)
er bellt (it barks)

The German subject pronouns are shown on the opposite page, with the verbs.

These are the direct object pronouns:

mich	me
dich	you
ihn	him, it(m)
sie	her, it(f)
es	it(n)
uns	us
euch	you
Sie	you (polite)
sie	them

e.g. *Ich rufe ihn* (I call him)

The indirect object pronouns are:

mir	me, to me
dir	you, to you
ihm	him, to him, it(m)(n), to it
ihr	her, to her, it(f), to it
uns	us, to us
euch	you, to you
Ihnen	you, to you (polite)
ihnen	them, to them

e.g. *Ich gebe ihr das Buch*
(I give her the book)

Possessive adjectives

The word you use for "my", "your", "his", etc., depends on whether the word that follows it is masculine, feminine, neuter or plural.

e.g. *mein Hund*(m) (my dog)
meine Blume(f) (my flower)
mein Kind(n) (my child)
meine Bücher(p) (my books)

	(m)	(f)	(n)	(p)
my	mein	meine	mein	meine
your	dein	deine	dein	deine
his, its(m)(n)	sein	seine	sein	seine
her, its(f)	ihr	ihre	ihr	ihre
our	unser	unsere	unser	unsere
your	ihr	ihre	ihr	ihre
your(polite)	Ihr	Ihre	Ihr	Ihre
their	ihr	ihre	ihr	ihre

Useful verbs

Remember that *du* (singular) and *ihr* (plural) are used only by close friends and children, and that *Sie*, spelt with a capital "S", is for speaking to anyone you don't know very well. The verbs *sein* and *haben* are used a lot because they help to form the different tenses of other verbs.

sein	**to be**
ich bin	I am
du bist	you are
er ist	he, it(m) is
sie ist	she, it(f) is
es ist	it(n) is
wir sind	we are
ihr seid	you are
Sie sind	you are (polite)
sie sind	they are

haben	**to have**
ich habe	I have
du hast	you have
er hat	he, it(m) has
sie hat	she, it(f) has
es hat	it(n) has
wir haben	we have
ihr habt	you have
Sie haben	you have (polite)
sie haben	they have

kommen	**to come**
ich komme	I come
du kommst	you come
er kommt	he, it(m) comes
sie kommt	she, it(f) comes
es kommt	it(n) comes
wir kommen	we come
ihr kommt	you come
Sie kommen	you come (polite)
sie kommen	they come

gehen	**to go**
ich gehe	I go
du gehst	you go
er geht	he, it(m) goes
sie geht	she, it(f) goes
es geht	it(n) goes
wir gehen	we go
ihr geht	you go
Sie gehen	you go (polite)
sie gehen	they go

können	**to be able to, can**
ich kann	I can
du kannst	you can
er kann	he, it(m) can
sie kann	she, it(f) can
es kann	it(n) can
wir können	we can
ihr könnt	you can
Sie können	you can (polite)
sie können	they can

mögen	**to like, want**
ich mag	I like
du magst	you like
er mag	he, it(m) likes
sie mag	she, it(f) likes
es mag	it(n) likes
wir mögen	we like
ihr mögt	you like
Sie mögen	you like (polite)
sie mögen	they like

Negatives

To make a verb negative, add *nicht* after the verb.

e.g. *Ich gehe nach Hause*
(I go home)
Ich gehe nicht nach Hause
(I do not go home)

Questions

To ask a question in German, put the subject of the sentence after the verb.

e.g. *Sie verkaufen Postkarten*
(You sell postcards)
Verkaufen Sie Postkarten?
(Do you sell postcards?)

Index

This index lists some words individually and some under group names, such as food. Where you will find the German for the indexed word, the page number is printed in *italics*, like this: *6*

Index of German words

This index lists some of the German words you might see on signs and notices. Look up the page reference to find out what they mean.